MANUAL 4

MEN

DEAN

In the beginning… Man thought he had it all.
Then a woman showed up and complicated it.
Now this is what you end up with.

This book was inspired by
LOLA.

INDEX

DEAN

This is a work of fiction. It is only the
misrepresentation of any and all men ever. I
wrote this on the belief that woman wanted a
manual for us men. Well this can and probably
will disillusion you even more by reading it. You
may gain a few insights but they are at your own
discretion.
I imply only that I wrote this for women
everywhere. I figured if you weren't getting a
good laugh every now and then you might and
this will probably give you a very good laugh. I
hope you enjoy it and don't let the cover hit you
in the butt on the way out.

WARNING!

This manual must be read in its entirety before any decision, opinions and/or preconceived notions can be formed. By failing to read this manual in its entirety and forming any opinions or decisions based on non-factual evidence can be misleading.

Due to the nature of man, no further guidance can be construed from this manual or any other currently or to be printed in any form. You have just witnessed the actual evidence that man is not a man but a being of and by itself. No man can be taken advantage of as described in the charter.

When you have maintained and read what this manual implies, you may have an idea of where man stands. No man was ever or can be evaluated by this manual for any intent purpose or reason. This can be the most fruitful and original book ever published or written and all user/owners must purchase this manual, before interacting with any model listed herein.

The user/owner may not be held accountable for any misrepresentation of any and all written words in this manual. The man is a wild beast and must be tamed according to all the charters listed herein, or in any manual written or to be written. It will be the responsibility of any user/owner to accept the man as he is. If you have received your man under false pretenses, then you may have purchased your man unsuccessfully.

When any user/owner reads this manual they may become enlightened or dizzy. It is then up to the user/owner to distinguish what is right and wrong for the model they have interacted with. Interacting with any model without this manual may be a violation of any charter listed.

Congratulations!
You have just purchased a manual that will possibly, maybe, somewhat come in handy for future endeavors. Some of the items listed within this manual may not be appropriate for any or all audiences. Not suitable for children under the age of 18. Some language may need to be monitored by parents. One of the many reasons some people buy this book are because they want a better understanding of what doesn't make a man tick, tock, or anything else for that matter.

This could be a very valuable asset when it comes to dealing with your not so run of the mill man. Some models do not adhere to any rules and may not be accountable at any time they are alone or with someone. While many just want a slight but not even close insight to the workings of a mans mind may cause irreparable damage to any user who actually tries to use this as a guidance tool.

There are many sides to any model within this manual. Some models vary by intelligence, sweetness, looks, likes, dislikes, moods, various sundries, behavior and anything that makes them different. We will delve not into the mind of any man known but instead to the regions most people don't know about. A region known only to you the user/owner. Of this we cannot tell what it is you are interpreting it as.

Upon completing and understanding all the contents of this manual, will you be better able to not so quite understand what a man is like. Ask yourself, do I really wanna know? Answer, of course. Why the heck not? Who really doesn't want to know what man might think in someone else's perspective of a mind I know not! Beware this manual may cause undue stress and problems. These problems are yours and you must make your own manual for your own model. If unable to do so because of a lack of mentality and compassion then you should not attempt any of these tricks, tips or anything else without prior consent of the model you are currently seeking to interact with.

If you have not consulted your local group for approval to interact with men, then you give up any claim or part of any claim or claim that may try to be brought against the writer or publisher or anyone else connected with this manual. This is intended for entertainment purposes only and can only be used for amusement only. Once you have purchased this manual there is no refund on anything.

All models contained within this manual are "AS IS" with no warranty implied here or at any time during the interaction process or lack thereof. All untagged models are virtually representative of all models contained within this manual. As this manual continues into the depths and minds of not many models or none at all, you will find out absolutely nothing except what you have already learned with hands on experience.

If you are interacting with only the intention of a 1-time interaction, then you must disclose this to the model for full disclosure before interacting. At no time can we provide any kind of assistance. All models contained within this manual are not free of defects or problems and many more may arise over the course of the agreement signed by both parties at the beginning of the interaction period. Any forms not signed and approved may constitute no or some local laws please see your local laws for further information.

Any questions that you may have during the process of reading this manual and understanding it, is totally and probably will always be misunderstood. Any questions you cannot answer yourself may be answered within a short period of time if given the chance to view the forms and documents that must be enclosed with all requests. Any and all requests can be sent to an address that is not possible to locate. For any other address that you may require please consult someone whom has the knowledge but cannot disclose for privacy purposes.

In this manual you may find answers and questions without answers. But rest assured as you read a new insight is born and you will begin to not quite understand what man and all models listed hereafter really are like and their intentions. If for some reason you feel you have purchased this manual under false pretenses, then you should pass it on to someone else. By reading this far you are now bound by the agreement which can be found on the agreement page. If agreement page is not found, one cannot be found at the store where a new manual may be purchased.

If purchasing a new manual, you may want to consult any and all people who have read or intend to read or maybe might one day get around to it for further input. If no one can be found, then you may purchase this manual and suffer what all users/owners go through when the interaction process begins.

This manual does not give the user the right to punish or cause to be punished any model they may interact with. As with any model you interact with, changes happen on an hourly scale. As these models interact more and more with a user/owner, they change to fit the needs and desires of the user/owner. In certain instances these changes activated the circuit known as a Digital Interactive Circuit Kicker. When activated this may cause other circuits and/or chips to go bad or cause to be bad. Some circuits may end up irreparable or unreplaceable.

No model may be or is ever trouble or glitch free. In this manual you may learn but not understand what a man can be like in true life. If that were possible you would have gotten this manual as soon as the time came to be. If this manual does not give you insight then you may have actually gotten to understand a man and you may have a glitch, which cannot be corrected at this time. Any model of human who is of earth born has glitches and problems. So no manual can give you full insight into any model ever made or to be made.

However there is possibly and maybe could be a new manual that may explain everything any human ever wanted to know about life and what we are. But if that is not available at time of publication or maybe never, then please feel free to make any decisions based on first hand experience. Most if not all models listed within this manual should not be taken for granted or assume anything. By doing this you will have activated the self-defense mechanism, which in some models may cause an urge to drive or evacuate the premises for a time until the modules can be reset.

Some models may not reset or it may require a longer time in which to reset or if you can actually activate the self reset chip which can only be accomplished by nothing or no one. That chip was found questionable and was not integrated into any model made after year 0001. Thank you and again Congratulations.

CAUTION
READ AT OWN RISK
Unofficial and not issued by any higher being

Disclaimer: This manual is possible and may be possible through talks with you know who. No men were harmed in the making of this book. Just after when women decided they wanted to throw the manual at the man for his ignorant, stupid and idiotic ways. The pages you are about to read may contain one or more errors and writer, publisher or anyone else involved in the making of this book is not responsible for any actions that may or possibly could lead to any harm coming to anyone other than oneself and then the reader is responsible for their own actions and interpretations.

By coming into contact with a model, you must always look and be a little shy but make the first move. Men like partners who want to take the lead once in a while at some point and possibly in the near future. But as a pre-caution, please be advised men are always unpredictable and totally out of sync with your type of life. Models who exhibit strange behavior may not be held responsible for any action they may cause or to be caused by any action of their own.

Any resemblance to anyone living or dead is pure coincidence and was thought up with possibly, maybe, I don't know the teachings of higher non-educational beings or entities. This manual is not intended as a guide to the inner workings of a real man. If this were a manual that were true and to the point then you couldn't afford it. This is just a generalized guide of some of the traits of men through my eyes and maybe others.

If you feel you bought this manual in error, it just goes to show you are not as intelligent as we might think you are. Some errors have been reported in certain models and may not be returned without sufficient sacrifice. While reading this manual you may want to consider your own evaluation of the model or models in question. Always remember men are only as complicated as you the user/owner can make them.

In case of an emergency with your man please contact whoever you need to, depending on the emergency. In case of glitches in modules or circuits please consult your nearest recall center. All recall centers are located within your mind and may be contacted through whatever means you deem necessary. If for any reason you feel jilted, unloved, used, abused, needy, wanting, ill, healthy, bad, good, or any other feeling, then you have totally misunderstood what this manual means. Absolutely nothing.

Some if not most of this manual covers some if any of the models for the Terra sector. If you live in a different sector you may have to purchase another manual for your sector. Sectors are zoned according to specifications not known to anyone outside the realm. The realm may consist of many structures and levels not yet determined.

MODELS COVERED

This manual covers models: For this example the name and birth date are John Allen Doe born December 25, 1974.

So this manual is for model J12A25D1974. First name initial, birth month, middle name initial, birth month day, last name initial, birth year.

All models covered unless tag has been removed then a different manual must be purchased separately and for a nominal processing fee, handling fee and shipping fees that will apply. Any warranty implied is null and void once tag has been removed.

AGREEMENT

For all intent purposes from hereon when male, men or model is used this manual is referring to the man. And from hereon the term user or owner is referring to the counterpart or other half.

The male model(s) contained within this manual may be more complicated and difficult than originally intended. Due to the extreme nature the male has undergone, some models may be controlling, abusive, cuddly, beeraholics, dopeheads, freaks, normal men, businessmen, funny men, asses, jerks, idiots, total losers, millionaires, poor men, middle income men, and just all men in general. By getting involved with any model, it is required to use caution.

Due to a glitch in the Testosterone Level Chip or TLC, some models may snap instantly and without provocation or without any idea of why they are doing what they are doing. Some models when a glitch happens may turn out to be a crybaby when sad movies are on. When this happens the Emotional Displeasure module or ED, (we know what that is, hint, hint), may not be sufficiently connected as originally intended. On these models there is no repair or fix for this problem. But some drugs may help depending on the mood of the model in question.

All models come with a manual. Any model without a manual may be a clone of the real model or they may have lost their manual or they weren't issued one because of a failure in our service. If your model didn't come with a manual you may want to purchase one before getting involved with models without manuals. There could be dire consequences if you get involved with a model that doesn't come with a Compatibility And Resource Engine or CARE module.

The male ego is by far the dumbest module available today. Almost all or some of the models have this and it was recalled but none have ever been returned. If you can provide adequate support and faith in any and all his possible abilities then you should get a model today, if you cannot then it is advisable to not interact or cause to interact with man. If for some reason you find yourself interacting and it feels good then that model may be the equivalent of what you are looking for. If not then you should never lead a man on with no intention of stimulating his mind as well as his outer shell.

Detailed user manuals may be available in some areas but not in any area where they can be bought. This may also have not been published or never intend to be published.

USE

The use of the model selected varies and this manual does not intend to give any tips or tricks unless otherwise stated. By using the model selected, you must abide by rules and regulations brought forth by the General Office of Discovery or GOD. There are certain use restrictions in most and many if not all places in the world. As with any machine not man made, they require special use permits for anything outside the normal rules and regulations. No examples follow.

By using any model it is up to the user/owner to determine what use the model selected is being intended for. All disclosures must be made in advance when underlying intentions are planned. In case of accidental slip and fallage, model in question is not responsible for any errors or problems that may arise due to a lack of self-control. On some but not quite all models, any disorientation may be fixed or repaired at your nearest service center. Please refer to Manual 3 EVERYTHING IN BETWEEN for any module, chip or terminator where these may be described in a questionable fashion.

After a limited time the further use of any model may require special permits which can be purchased separately from another manual not yet written. Please be patient as we address this problem in the not to near future. The use of any model constitutes problems and errors when interaction is taken. Any problems or errors caused by this model are not the responsibility of any model at any time.

Some models when used in conjunction with other models may activate a jealousy chip. If this happens, contact your emergency service center, which cannot be found. If you successfully find the emergency service center, please respect our privacy and don't tell anyone where it may be located.

Using some models too much may cause serious side effects, which can be located in the pre-caution section of this manual. If for some reason the side effects are not available at time of printing, you may purchase the side effects pamphlet at your nearest service center. By using any model you may be required to pay a small user's fee if applicable. By using any model before reading any manual or book, models cannot be held accountable for any action they cause or cause to be caused.

Some models when in use may cause a short circuit at any given time depending on the model and type and life span integrated into the action or lazy chip. When this happens do not panic. It is normal. All models eventually get this chip activated. Let the model do as it wishes for an approximate amount of time. Time varies with models listed or ever to be listed. You may use any model in dry, wet, clean, dirty, normal, abnormal, high, low, deep, and shallow or any other condition unless tagged otherwise.

Be firm yet gentle when using any model. If you use this model in any conditions listed or not listed then it is up to the user/owner to care and maintain for this model. Poor maintenance on part of user may violate one or more local laws depending on the world you currently reside in. Do not use any model in any condition listed anywhere in this manual or in any other currently in print or ever to be in print.

All models when used according to all guidelines and rules and regulations may or may not meet all regulations by local authorities. Any model used outside the user/owner area may violate some rules that are not covered in any manual anywhere or ever to be printed in any form. Some models may be used for money if model in question agrees by signing any document placed in front of said model.

You may use any model for any reason or purpose not related to personal interaction or inaction on the part of the user/owner. If model is used for any personal reasons then all models and user/owners must sign the agreement. If interaction has started before agreement is signed then all warranties are null and void and will not be honored at any service center. Using any model outside said zones constitutes violations located within this manual or maybe a manual not yet printed or to be printed.

When any model is used in the manner it was designed to be used, then any or most all models listed or unlisted may fall under one or more or less of the following listed warranties available at any dealer located within your area.

If no dealer can be located then you must have purchased a used model. All used models have no warranty or implied warranty of any type or kind.

When using any model for entertainment and/or personal use be cautious of what any and all models ingest. Some models and or all not listed here or before this point may be equipped with the General Alert System chip or GAS. When activated this model will send out a general alert via escaping odoriferous emissions from any and all orifices where they may escape. Some if not all models listed or unlisted may or may not be equipped with this chip.

Using any model without regard for their safety may violate or cause to violate some if any local or unlocal laws somewhere in the galaxy. Any and all models must be involved when any party bases decisions on false or fraudulent misrepresentation. Special Use permits are available for any model. To purchase said permits please see a local service center where they can be purchased for a nominal fee.

Using any model for more than 5 hours at one time may activate the Tranquilized Individual Response Emergency Diagnostic or what is most commonly called the TIRED chip. When activated model(s) may exhibit yawn-like behavior and/or any of the other ailments associated with this chip.

When using any model a flip chip may be activated. All models come equipped with this bad boy. When activated this chip just happens to make the model flip any module, terminator or chip in reverse. In other words a good chip goes bad. Or worse. This chip can activate any and all modules, terminators or chips in any model and could also adversely affect other nearby models.

Please, use the model you have with respect, admiration, loyalty, dedication, honesty and above all love. All models have a guilt circuit. When activated by user/owner causes any model to instantly enter a defensive position. This circuit is activated by the mood of user/owners. When user/owner is upset, the circuit completes and the activation begins. Once activated this circuit is hard to close down. Usually takes 1 to 3 days depending on model you have.

DO NOT use any models once the guilt circuit is activated. Once activated it could cause undue and serious consequences to one or all of its internal parts. No model is exempt and if you purchased your model with this already activated no warranty is implied and no recalls are available.

Once the user/owner of any model exceeds any time limit given by any part of this manual, then an impress chip may possibly be activated. Once activated it cannot be de-activated or terminated by any means other than leaving said model(s) at nearest location where it was purchased. Once purchased, you cannot return to any given location, except those specified by the previous manual over-rides.

Some models when used may provide inadequate comfort at times when user/owner may need a shoulder to lean on. Any user/owner who may happen to cry in the presence of a masculine model may be shunned or treated as a leper. If this happens you may want to trade your model in for a more emotionally supported model. On any model if used while being overly protective may exhibit some trauma-related experiences from childhood. If this happens you may inadvertently be involved with an unsupported model.

MAINTENANCE

Maintenance is required on all models unless otherwise specified or stated herein. Depending on model some require hourly maintenance. Some require daily maintenance or even long term maintenance. Long term maintenance is a rare model and must be found by using your heart and soul as guidance. Some of these may even be thrown back if not acceptable in its current format. For these models an extra expense is required at additional cost to the owner.

No model if any is maintenance free. As with all models there always resides the current maintenance check. This check must be performed at any time it is deemed necessary by any model who is not of the same series but must contain a certain appearance to said model. If regular maintenance is not kept up, then any model may actively seek a user/owner who is willing to abide by the Manual 4 Men.

All models found outside any area where it is prohibited may be reported to the nearest service center. Some if not all service centers require a nominal non-refundable and sizable down payment. Due to poor returns after making said deposits, most user/owners never returned. This fee covers all accounting and personal required to address any issue the user/owner may have.

Maintenance guides are useful but have never been published before or after the publication of this manual. Some manuals may have been issued with these guides but may not be available at time of publication. At no time shall any maintenance guides be available for any model. Maintenance issues do arise so if your model needs maintenance then it is up to the user/owner to perform maintenance requirements.

Some models may come with certain disability features, which must be evaluated prior to interaction. Unintentional errors that cause or cause to be caused to any model from any user/owner or model(s) is not responsible for any actions that caused failures to any models, in, around or near other model(s). Any model that requires multiple service checks daily will be left up to the discretion of the user/owner. There could or may be an update available for any model not listed here or in any other manual. EXTREME CAUTION: If any model is of the smoking and/or coffee drinking kind, DO NOT converse with any model prior to one or both of these activities.

Maintenance schedules vary by model. Below is an example of a possible maintenance schedule.

4:30 a.m. Wake model up interactively.
5:00 a.m. Make models lunch for the day.
5:30 a.m. allow any model to watch local news or anything they require.

6:00 a.m. Kiss model bye and say you love him.
4:00 to 6:00 p.m. Have dinner made and kiss
model when entering the front, back and/or side
door(s).

After this time any maintenance required can
be done somewhat successfully by any
user/owner. You must have passed by at least
10% the required maintenance program
available in many places not controlled by any
government. Maintenance schedules vary by
model design and functions. Please consult a
professional for further assistance.

Some if any maintenance can or may be
performed after any model is in recharge mode.
Use caution as some models have been
reported to have unusual motions if awakened
by slightest noise, feel or touch. On these
models use extreme caution if any maintenance
plans are being done during this time.

Some maintenance may require special tools
and/or custom fit products available at some if
any store or outlet currently open in the service
center(s) in your area. During routine
maintenance inspection, (which must be done
according to any guidelines currently in print or
ever to be printed), if you encounter any
problems you must repair them immediately. By
not addressing any inspection report, you could
possibly or even maybe cause or cause to be
caused violation(s) of some areas not affiliated
with any of our organizations which do not exist.

Any maintenance performed by any
unauthorized user/owners may constitute
violation of model in question. All maintenance
must be performed by an authorized service
center. Some if any maintenance may be done

by any user/owner who works at an authorized
service center. Maintenance not required may be
listed in another section of a manual not yet
published. Maintenance must be performed
according to guidelines and if any maintenance
is not performed or problems are not addressed,
then any model with a valid warranty will be null
and void.

Few if any require long-term maintenance.
On these models maintenance can and might
possibly be done by the model in question,
provided they are equipped with a self-diagnostic
system only available for limited times as listed
in a different publication not yet available. As
with all maintenance issues, some should be
reported and any not reported may constitute
some kind of violation somewhere at sometime.

Any issues that may arise from failure to do
proper maintenance on any model may result in
unusual and distressing behavior with some
models. Some models may also exhibit strange
moods or distant behavior not supported by this
manual. Some and most all models have
maintenance issues at least once a day. When
these times occur, user/owner must give free
reign to model unless otherwise specified
anywhere else in this manual or any other.

If during any maintenance inspection or repair
user/owner is unable to finish repair said model
might be brought in for assistance. For
assistance in these matters, please consult
MANUAL 3 EVERYTHING IN BETWEEN. Any
unauthorized repair manual, which may be in
print and if not then you should purchase one
when and if they become available.

Maintenance should be performed when model(s) are in modes before or after this tip which could possibly be maybe found somewhere else. If any maintenance is performed and model(s) malfunctions severely, them said model(s) are exempt from any further association with any user/owner that may try to over ride model(s) sense circuit.

When sense circuit is activated any and all possibly more model(s) may become disoriented or may become unstable. Evacuate said perimeter where diagram is located near a page with no number as prescribed in a different manual. DO NOT try to ignore any model(s) when and if they ever get depressed, happy, sad, moody, sleepy, awake, driving, working or any other event any and all model(s) may do.

Additional maintenance schedules may be available at some service centers.

CARE

Please read all tags for care and maintenance information. If tag is missing please contact your local GODthority for further assistance. In some cases there may not be sufficient information from which to give accurate or intelligent information that may possibly somewhat be available at the time of inquiry. As with all models these models must be cared for and attended to at most all times when not alone. Pampering is required as long as friends of this model are not present or soon to be present. When certain models are out for entertainment with friends, they must not be contacted unless it is an emergency only. Some models require definitive contact and visual enhancements.

When first engaging with any model you must use extreme caution. No model has ever been correctly integrated or in tune with any female model. No model has undergone any kind of therapy unless forced into it after birth. Models with glitches are listed here: ALL

If you feel the model you selected isn't worth your time or money, then these models must be returned to the market where they were purchased and told it is over. By doing this you may inadvertently trigger an unknown response. Extreme care is best used in these circumstances. All models must be attended to and told many times that they are great. If any model is working on a project you must tell the model every hour what a great job they are doing.

If the model you have selected requires additional care, you must have them treated before triggering their Emotional And Timely module or EAT, as it may cause grave consequences for the model in question. If loss of weight occurs you must return and make them better before continuing your search for the next model. No model must be left in worse condition than when you found them.

When ill the model in question may require extreme attention from the user. You must never call them babies or lazy while in this condition. By causing anguish or mental strain on an ill model may result in consequences from your local GODthority. The use of the model you selected makes the user responsible for any care or cleaning required. Some models may have a self-interest chip and in these cases please feel free to call your local service center for any questions you may have.

Some models equipped with the Electronic Genetic Organ or EGO which is most if not all models of various sizes and shapes. When this module is activated, which happens when the model in question was first understandable of any knowledge and good feelings, causes a new glitch in certain other modules, chips or terminators. When this happens, be calm and do as the model says.

Eventually you will get out or the EGO chip may malfunction. In this event distance yourself until the chip has reset itself. If chip fails to reset you may return any model to a service center anywhere near you! All service centers are open every day of every year and never close.

Additional care instructions could possibly be found on the backside of the original tag that came with your model. If unable to locate please feel free to call a service center for replacement documentation. Some models may require additional care when using more than 1 model at a time. If more than one model is purchased user/owner must purchase a special permit for the use of more than 1 model at one time. These permits can be found at your local service center.

When caring for your model, please make sure you clean all moving parts as well as non-moving parts, which can collect dirt and debris and could possibly cause distress with your model. If you have purchased the extended care warranty, you will want to avoid any unforeseeable accidents, which may and can occur at any time during use. No user/owner may use any extended care benefits without first applying for said benefits after the successful purchase of extended benefits.

The official care online forum may not be available in your area. Some areas require additional costs to log on or use the services it may contain. These care services are for legal user/owners with proper documentation. Some documentation requires additional fees or charges that do not have to be disclosed until after services are performed on any model.

Any products you may have purchased with your model may not be legal in most places not exactly known where the location is actually located. Some locations vary by model purchased. Some models require more care than others, due to high volume and low quality models. Older models with reliable parts may be more reliable than current models. Newer models may have more defects due to high prices and new technology that makes it more complicated to find any model desired.

Quality models are easier to care for and tend to have fewer problems than their current model counterparts. Easier care can be acquired through a pay as you go plan. Nominal service charges and exorbitant fees may and will apply to all transactions. Any and all agreements to this will be automatically enrolled in the life plan. With this plan you are covered for life provided you don't get rid of model being covered. Payments will be withdrawn at the first business day of the first four weeks of every month not to exceed 500% of user/owners income. Some models cannot be covered with this plan.

Optional care upgrades can be purchased with additional fees and extra charges. These charges and fees may and will be charged regardless of service provided if any was provided at time of order. Some orders will not be processed due to restrictions or limitations without notice to any user/owner involved. Any model covered under any of the plans in this manual cannot be combined or used in conjunction with any coupon you may find.

Coupons are not valid for care products or
services. Coupons are only good during the
warranty period of your model.

In the event you can no longer care for your
model, you may be required to turn said model
back in for reprocessing at the nearest center
available. The manufacturer of said model(s)
must endorse all care services and products.
Any model(s) not covered for this will be notified
via mail if said model is under warranty. In no
event can any model fall under any warranty or
extended care plans for any model in question.

When care services can be provided for
nominal fees and charges, all user/owners will
be notified in the event their model may happen
to be covered. Care for your model must be
maintained and kept in a healthy manner in
accordance with the guidelines set in this
manual. Cautious care must be provided around
vital areas to keep them clean and free of any
and all defects that may occur.

Care is mandatory in most cases where
model(s) can be accessed during certain times
in which the model(s) may not be comfortable
during said care services provided by
user/owners.

RULES AND REGULATIONS

The following rules and regulations pertain to all models unless otherwise specified.

You must tell this unit he is right at least once a week. Morale Booster

You must not leave this model alone for any extended periods. Depression Module may be activated if left alone for too long.

All models require at least a minimum of 1 hour of alone time daily. Some models may require longer alone times, please see special precautions if your model is equipped with the extended function modules.

You must always kiss and say I love you when this model leaves for any outing or excursion.

When certain models are acquired, some modules may be defective and must be handled accordingly.

Some models require daily cleansing and may have to be told at times to do this but not in a mean way.

Some models require romantic interludes at least once a week at any or no predetermined time and day.

Most models require special toys and tools. To find out if your model has any of these special TT modules, see tag.

All models are upgraded or downgraded according to lifestyle, habits, interests and any actions that may cause temporary or permanent alterations to it's internal programming.

When model or models covered by this manual thinks with something other than its brain or heart, then it is up to the user/owner to interpret such actions before they become a problem for the user/owner.

All models require special handling. With these models please refer to another manual purchased separately.

No model must be given free reign to do as they please. By allowing this the Emotional Trauma Chip or ETC may cause unintentional or dire consequences upon user/owner in question.

Some models may require special guidance when in doubt of the right answer.

When the Idiot Chip Emitter or ICE occurs, the model(s) listed may not be responsible for any and/or all actions that cause them to just stand there and look at you all stupid like. They may even have that glazed look as if their brain weren't capable of processing that thought.

In some instances some or most all models may experience shopping trauma. When this occurs you must buy them a toy immediately. Something shiny and bright.

When any model looks at or says anything about anything electronic, toolwise, appliances or any other item that could possibly be mentioned does not mean that they require it or want it at that time.

Some if not all models have problems with wiring and plumbing. If your model has a problem please consult manufacturer for more assistance. If you don't know who the manufacturer may be, please call our customer service line at your convenience.

Some models may be equipped with a Delayed Integrated Module With Instant Termination or a DIMWIT. If so equipped and activated by user, the user is responsible for model actions that seem out of place or not quite them.

Freedom rule. Any model covered by this manual has the freedom to make it's own choices and decisions provided user/owner has given permission. If not, then no model may be covered by any manual published today.

Any rule or regulation before or beyond this point is not really a rule or regulation at all.

Any chore/job that any model may forget to do or just doesn't do becomes the responsibility of the user/owner.

UPON COMPLETION OF SUCCESSFUL TARGETED DATES AS LISTED
6 MONTHS

Congratulations, you did it. You are well on your way towards full ownership. The first 6 months are said to be some of the most important. As we delve further into the next set of dates, you will find new challenges that await you. As with all models challenges are a part of their programming.

1 YEAR

Way to go. You did it this time. Now you are getting closer to the final date. Think of it as a game at this point. All models like some or not all of the games as they are played. Rules must apply to all parties concerned. By this time you should be living together and learning all the new, neat things you will need if you plan on a future with your model. If you are not residing together at this time, then you may have a Delayed Unit Module Brain model or DUMB model.

3 YEARS

Almost there and still going strong. By this time you should be married and totally into each other. Some models require children in models of various makes and sizes.

5 YEARS

Have a party, you finally did it. This is the critical date. When you have successfully reached this date, the user is totally responsible for any action that said model does, did or is going to do.

Any rule or regulation not covered in this manual may be added later by the user/owner. However, just because it was added does not make it any part of this manual. Any and all or part of this manual may change at any time without prior notice. Rules change daily and no updates are available at this time. Changes by any user/owner is forbidden and constitutes higher violation of laws. No violation will go punished. All violations can be found in the violation section of a book that doesn't exist.

Some rules and regulations are not allowed to be followed in certain conditions. These certain conditions for model(s) in question can be found in Manual 9: Addendum and Reference. If you cannot find this Manual please contact your local service center. If all rules and regulations are followed and model becomes unstable or erratic, consult appropriate authorities in your area as to the nature of the model and its condition. These authorities may also be found at the extended service centers located in one of many different locations.

ADDITIONAL RULES AND REGULATIONS

As with any and all rules and/or regulations, these must be followed and never veered from. Any user/owner who violates and/or breaks these rules and regulations may be responsible for anything the current model in question does, will do and/or may do at any time either previous to current user/owner taking interactive interest or after any use.

1. Physical, Emotional or Mental abuse or any combination thereof:

No user shall violate or cause to be violated any of the abuses listed

If any abuse is present, then user/owner must show proof they did not cause any of the abuses as listed unless otherwise stated.

Mental abuse must be used in conjunction with emotional abuse.

No Physical abuse may be tolerated without all abuses being inflicted upon model in question.

If any model suffers from any abuse they may be relieved of any and all encumbrances upon them

2. Trauma and results thereof:

No model may be responsible for the actions of any user/owner who causes trauma to any model.

Trauma can be the results of unforeseen complications that may arise during any time of the models period of activity.

If any trauma befalls any model during any use or non-use in whole or in part may violate any or all of the following and previous rules and regulations.

Any trauma that any model may experience is always caused by current user/owner and will be held responsible for any reason deemed necessary under all guidelines listed or to be listed.

Thinking and changes thereof:

No change may be made to any model regardless of user/owner status.

When model in question has a thought no user/owner may interpret it as anything other than what may have been intended by model.

3. Pets, limitations and responsibilities:

When any model requires any pet or animal they take no responsibility for their care and maintenance.

User/owner is responsible for any and all care for any pet/animal any and all models require or need for special requirements not listed in this manual.

Farmers and scientists may be exempt from any of these requirements. If you have one of these models, no user/owner may interfere, hinder or in any way impede said model(s) from any special requirements they may have been installed with. To see this list see section 56 paragraph 45

Limitations of operability and the exclusions, thereof:

Some models with certain restrictions may not be operated in unfriendly manners or ways which may harm or cause to be harmed any model in question.

Some models not listed may not be operated under any of the following conditions;

Cloudy days, rainy days, clear days, sunny days, snow days, hot days, cold days or any days where a sun may be present or moon or both in any combination.

Any and all models excluded from this regulation can be found in any other section not related to any model.

Maintaining and keeping a healthy model, and any exclusions thereof:

Models in the category as found on page 3 of the worksheet guidelines may be exempt from any and all exclusions.

No model may be self-maintained.

On all models except as noted, may require special tools and toys and/or the acquirization of items that may be of special interest.

Duties and limitations of any and all responsibilities:

No model will be required to spend any time with any user/owner who acquires them unnaturally.

All models are required to perform any duty that is not in violation of any and all rules or regulations.

Some models may be limited in any responsibility they agree to with any user/owner.

No user/owner may limit any duty or responsibility unless otherwise noted.

RECALLS

Most all of the models covered by this manual have been recalled for possibly, maybe, I don't know one fault or another. Due to the low demand of recalls we may be out having fun. With no recalls coming in we might as well enjoy life. If you are too busy to come in and have your recall serviced, then we are too busy to help you. Some recalls may be repaired on site. For this information you may call any service center for the number to the mobile service repair specialist at any time.

Some recalls, which may have been repaired, are not the responsibility of any service center or repair technician. No technician may be held responsible for any malfunctioning module that may have been inadvertently activated. By refusing to bring your model in for any recall or maintenance may result in voiding the warranty if any model had one. Some models not covered by this book may be warranteed for as long as you own your model.

01-01-0001   TSB Recall   Defective GAS chip   Recall notice TBD   This chip was found defective after installing it in almost some of the models and/or all models. This chip by malfunctioning causes outbursts of odoriferous emissions at any and possibly all times whether awake or asleep, living or dead.

01-02-0001   TSB Recall   Defective EGO chip   recall Notice Ayt65776   This chip was found to over-inflate at unusual times and places. Over-indulging models may cause this chip to malfunction prematurely. Too much praise and the model(s) may be unstoppable when it comes to loving itself. Use caution if these chips haven't been repaired or replaced with new chips.

01-04-0002   TSB Recall   Defective or Missing ATTITUDE module Recall Notice Yttr87987667   This module may have been inadvertently on back order at time of construction of any model missing this item. If module malfunctions serious consequences may and could possibly follow.

PHRASES

Usually after 3 months and longer, the TLC chip activates the Automatic Response Chip or ARC. By activating, the most responses you will get after it has been activated will be as follows and what they mean when said;

EXAMPLE 1: Question; How much spaghetti do you want Baby? REPLY; Oh so-so which means usually not too much but enough that I don't have to get my lazy ass up and get more.

EXAMPLE 2: Question; Do these jeans make my butt look big? Reply; Nooo said kind of sincerely which means Nooo...your butt was already big but I can't say that.

EXAMPLE 3: Question; Do you love me Baby? Reply; of course I do baby, which means depending on how it was said.

Honestly means yes he does but as with all models there is the possibility of a glitch in the system and it could mean he doesn't but makes you believe he does.

Says it with some caution which means yes he possibly might maybe love you but maybe not in the way you may possibly think or take it.

Says it but doesn't seem to sound like it and he doesn't even look at you, means yes he does but as with all models there is the possibility of a glitch at any given time, day, night, week, month or year.

The following examples are not intended to guide you or give you any insight into the actual workings of a man. You may refer to any book you can find which has the information you are looking for and then make your judgement on what you might think men really are like and what they want.

EXAMPLE A: Man is watching a show and really likes it. The user/owner asks a question which the man did not hear. Do not take this as a snub or I wasn't listening. Just wait for a damn commercial.

EXAMPLE B: When driving, do not do the driving from the passenger seat. It distracts us. Now you know why we need something shiny and bright hanging from the rear view mirror. To distract us from you.

EXAMPLE C: Food

1. So-so means some but not too much.
2. A little means a little more than so-so but not as much as you think.
3. Some means I am kind of hungry but still aren't sure how hungry.
4. More than a little means give it to me but don't expect me to eat it all.

The above may contain unsuitable commands for certain models. Above may only be used as a guide and again we are not responsible for any misuse of this manual not outlined.

In some and possibly most cases almost all of the models available have been known to use the phrase, "I Don't Know" quite often. When any user/owner is replied by the model using this phrase in most cases but select few means that they just don't know. It doesn't mean they forgot or that they should be evaluated. If for some reason you hear this often then your model may either be defective or some module or chip or circuit may have been inadvertently triggered due to a user/owner flaw.

SPECIAL PRECAUTIONS

The Extended Functions Module is designed for the sportsman, adventurer, businessman and any model that requires extended alone times for special intervention either alone or with a group of men capable of performing the same extended functions.

When the Automatic Threat Transducing Independent Timed Universal delayed Emitter module or ATTITUDE is activated no one assumes responsibility except the user/owner who caused it to be activated. Responses vary from model to model. No model may be harmed with this activated. All personal use models are equipped with this important module. If your model does not come equipped with this module or it may have mal-functioned, (which is not the responsibility of the maker of said model), must be returned immediately to the nearest service center you find.

When this model breaks down or malfunctions, the responsibility falls into the hands of the user/owner of the model to fix or repair and in some cases replace the model with a newer updated model or it could be a downgraded model. Any issues you find during your interaction process must be reported immediately. Any failure to do so may or will not kind of result in any kind of legal action against user/owner.

Trade in value can sometimes cost you, the user/owner, a fee in certain cases. There have been a reported few if any at all where a fee is not charged. Most fees charged are given to any psychoanalyctical model not listed in this manual. If model is listed then a typographical error has occurred and we cannot be held responsible for any errors or typographical errors contained within this manual.

Trauma or severe injury or even death by the user can result in punishment, fines and even death in some cases. Please see local laws for more information. If you feel the information given was insufficient to successfully interact with any model listed here, then you may require MANUAL 3; (this manual may not be available at time of publication). MANUAL 3 may or may not be published in the not near or distant future.

If you feel you have gained invaluable knowledge from this manual then you misinterpreted it. Please be advised that total misrepresentation of any or all or any part of this manual, releases the writer, publisher and anyone else connected with this manual from any and all legal action or recourse. In the event that all pre-cautions and rules and/or regulations were followed this in no way allows any kind of recourse or legal action.

POSSIBLE SIDE EFFECTS CONTAINING ONE OR MORE OF THE FOLLOWING SYMPTOMS

Side effects of any and all models are as follows: Dizziness, vomiting, diarrhea, choking, cramps, bloating, weight gain, weight loss, attitude, blood from nose, may also bleed from eyes or ears, ringing sound, instability, disorientation, uncontrollable movements, singing off-key, swelling of the feet or hands, excessive drinking, frequent urination, constipation, stupor, idiotic stare, total stupidity, ignorant behavior and any action the model may exhibit.

If the model you have has any of these symptoms, they should be returned immediately for re-orientation. Some models may not have any symptoms and in this case you may be at fault. Most all models have flaws and side effects that are not required for interaction.

Any model with side effects of 2 or more of the above may be unstable and unfit for interaction. Most all the models available today may have 6 or more flaws and or side effects as described in Manual 3 Everything In Between. This may be purchased separately if so desired and if your model has persistent problems with any of the above mentioned side effects.

Side effects are for dramatization purposes only and there may be other side effects not mentioned. If your model has any side effect that is not mentioned you have a model that has been recalled and may be returned where found. Some side effects may be attitude related and you should consult your manual for further information regarding this chip/module.

DISCLAIMER PAGE

By interacting with this model, you give up all rights to a peaceful life and existence. There is no warranty and none is implied. These models come with no warranty and imply no warranty in any advertising or circular you may have got. Warranty is upon successful birth. These models may or may not have skills or traits

By buying this manual you agree to all the terms and conditions listed herein and take full responsibility for any and all actions this model may cause or cause to happen through actions or inaction's on there part. Failure to abide by these conditions as set herein can be punishable by laws or regulations in your place of residence outside the zones marked unclearly in any section of this manual.

This manual is not intended to diagnose or treat the model you have purchased. This manual implies no fixes or repairs to any model. Some models will not be officially authorized to be available for any interactions resulting in the misdeeds of any model(s) involved with user/owners and/or non-user/owners.

Some models are equipped with a faulty desire module. On these models the product was recalled but none have ever been returned. No part of this manual may be misconstrued as anything other than entertainment. If any user/owner and/or model misrepresents any of the contents of this manual, it then becomes the sole responsibility of the party misconstruing the intention of this manual.

No person(s) involved with the making of this manual may agree or disagree with any part without first contacting the proper representative in your area. Some people involved with the making may be in agreement with all or part of this manual except where stated at any other place in this manual.

As is with most cases, any and/or all model(s) listed in this manual are used fictitiously and are not intended to violate any rights of any individuals who feel they may be harmed in the making of this manual. No actual models were harmed or hurt in the making of this manual. Additionally no user/owners were harmed or hurt either. Any models or user/owners who feel they were harmed or hurt may show proof to the courts at the end of the journey you have already embarked upon.

SPECIAL INSTRUCTIONS WHEN LOOKING FOR THE PERFECT MODEL

Make a list of traits, special interests, looks, likes, dislikes, eye color, hair color, hair style, tattoos, no tattoos, piercing(s), no piercing(s), facial ticks and/or scars, height, weight, attitude and any internal feelings you may require. Please submit all information above and below as well:

Photo ID
Social Security Number
Birth certificate
Current employer
Recent pay stub or copy thereof
All credit card account numbers and access codes
Current photo (must be taken within 1 week of submission of these documents.

A $77.70 plus shipping and handling fee of $7.77, sales tax is collected by your local government. All payments must be made in the form of anything that is usable where he resides.

Send all above to: GOD
1 Heaven Way
Lord Lane
Planetwide

00001

Please allow up to 1 day, (GOD time*) for
processing.

* GOD time is measured using biblical time
references. 1 GOD day is the equivalent of 10
million years or more. The current format serves
only to be used as a possible guide for reference
purposes only and not to be construed as
anything valid.

TROUBLESHOOTING

In this section we will attempt to troubleshoot any issues the user/owner may have regarding their model. Remember this is only a guide and cannot be used as a real troubleshooter or problem solver. If you would call customer service they can provide you with a number of a customer based service center somewhere besides where you might possibly be and where people don't exist. Please feel free to call any time, day or night. Phone lines are open 24 hours a day and forever. Phone lines do not close and cannot be disconnected. Some phone calls may be monitored for quality purposes.

For a current list of phone numbers in your area, please consult the book titled phone numbers in your area, (not yet released and may never be but just keep an eye out and we will to). Starting with finding which model you have, please refer to the book titled 'Interactive Labeling Lessons'. Kind of makes you ILL just thinking about it. Once you have found what the book has shown you, please move on to step 2.

Step 2: Please refer to step 1 for any questions regarding the rest of the questions.

Step 1: There are no questions as there is no way to troubleshoot any model you may encounter. All models come with a troubleshooter free warranty. This warranty is void in all states except where exempt models are listed. Please refer to another book, which has no title for this information.

Any other steps required will be sent to all user/owners when they become available. As models change and vary in a wide variety of differences and traits, new updated troubleshooting tips and tricks may be available for any model covered under any of the following and previous agreements.

Any and all problems resulting from any user/owner misuse of troubleshooting tips and tricks or rules must be reported to a supervisor in a service center in your area. Tip #3 Duality chips and their lesser functions. When activated these models will become someone else for a limited time as allotted in previous sections. There are no troubleshooting tips or tricks for these models. Any person in authority does not authorize troubleshooting tips and tricks and some techniques.

Any model that may come with certain upgrade features cannot be troubleshot at home or at any service center. Only extreme high clearance technicians are the only ones capable of troubleshooting any of the models that have these features. As of today no technicians are available, as it is hard to find any monkeys capable of thinking this low.

As the model you chose continues to be a good and helpful man, then any troubleshooting you find necessary may be bought with another policy available exclusively at any service center in your area. Some areas may not be covered if there is no service center. Once the comfort chip is activated no user/ owner may submit any model to anything they would not normally do on their own.

Another way to troubleshoot your model is by activating the models inner voice. When model is in sleep mode user/owners may ask questions but the answers may not be forthcoming or what was intended. This activates the inner troubleshooter and some or all models may be activated in this way.

As with anything made, problems do arise and troubleshooting is your best friend if used right. Some and most all user/owners may have not been properly educated in that field. For educational information and to take troubleshooting tips, tricks and home repair remedies please refer to another manual not described here. If troubleshooting problems don't help, your model may be defective and require immediate emergency assistance.

Troubleshooting numbers vary by location and may not be available in your area. As with any service all troubleshooting calls will be monitored for quality and customer assurance. Additional fees will apply when making any troubleshooting calls. Some calls will be received in the order they were made and others first. If you cannot find any help in this limited edition version of manual 4 men's troubleshooting section, then you may have to find another version, which may cover more information and troubleshooting techniques and/or tips and tricks.

Many and most all models will have no troubleshooting techniques available. If this is one of your models, then you may have inadvertently bought a used unlicensed model. If this is the case please contact a service center immediately. When notified they will send out an emergency license creator which if the model is licensable will be issued a license and given to the user/owner.

If user/owner is not available or the model has no user/owner then the license may be held at a different location than described where it might be found.

During troubleshooting you may find yourself feeling slightly shaky and nervous but anxious all at once. If you have these feelings you may be closer to finding an unlicensed model in your presence. Without further delay, you must take these models to any supervisor at any and/or all of the service centers. Do not confuse lust, love or unlicensed models as the feeling may be the same in all or some of all the instances.

When and if troubleshooting fails or is not correctly activated, user/owner may be responsible for all and any repairs needed to bring said model up to date. You will be charged accordingly during any troubleshooting phone calls. If you need help troubleshooting, troubleshooting please call the new unlisted number located in the front of every service center.

By troubleshooting, troubleshooting you may inadvertently trigger an unwanted side effect. In this case there is no hope of troubleshooting any model. Some but not quite any have these trigger switches and each response varies by make and/or model. Some models may require extra time for troubleshooting purposes.

As of 10-11-0012 the troubleshooting section may have been removed due to technical glitches and/or hackers. When troubleshooting is back up, user/owners will be notified via some kind of mail only men can think up. When the troubleshooting section fails to give accurate information for your model, you may have bought the wrong manual.

If you have bought the wrong manual please return to where you bought and buy the other one that may cover the model you have interacted with. In this case the interactivity violates the laws of the charter which is not accessible by any means human or otherwise. If you buy a manual with troubleshooting tips and/or tricks and/or techniques you may have bought an illegal copy. You are now a pirate.

This manual is intended for entertainment purposes only. Any models actually covered by this manual are not covered. There are no models covered, as there are no models available. The misuse or misunderstanding of the user/owner reading this manual is not the responsibility of the manual or its makers/creators. By reading this manual you hereby give up any rights for legal action or recourse.

This manual is not responsible for any typographical errors or any actions that may cause or cause to be any actions and/or activity that local, state and/or federal laws prohibit.

No models were injured, harmed or humiliated by the divulgence of this vital information. Any model that may feel one of these should seek some kind of professional help. No writer, publisher or anyone else involved in the making of this manual is responsible for any of the contents in whole or in any part. Any misunderstanding of the information contained in this manual is not intended to further any education for any person living or dead.

UNLICENSED MODELS

If you have bought or interacted with an unlicensed model, please report them immediately to any supervisor within a service center. There have been reports of unlicensed models infiltrating the models that are legit. On unlicensed models there will be no tag. These models need to be reported and tagged properly by the proper officials.

On most any and all models there may be a tag warning of said model being unlicensed. If tag has been removed you may attempt the troubleshooting section and troubleshoot said model in sleep mode. If this doesn't work you may be sleeping with an unlicensed and undeclared model. In these cases, most have reported problems with their models.

Below is a list of possible unlicensed models you may encounter. If you encounter any of these models please seek immediate help from any service center emergency task force. Unlicensed models are as follows:
1. Bald   2. Hairy   3. Tall   4. Slim   5. Big
6. White skin   7. Black skin   8. Brown skin
9. Green skin   10. Yellow skin   11.
Overweight   12. Underweight   13. Some or

all teeth   14. No teeth   15. Dentures   16. Partials   17. Young   18. Old   19. Middle aged   20. Brown eyes   21. Blue eyes   22. Black   23. Green   24. Amber   25. Blind 26. Perfect vision   27. Some vision   28. Smokers   29. Non-smokers   30. Drinkers 31. Comedians   32. Actors   33. Workers 34. Lazy bums   35. Homeless   36. Rich 37. Poor

Some of the models may be of such genuine manufacture you would never know. These are imitation men. They cannot be trusted to do anything worthwhile. Some if not all of these models may be verbally non-responsive to any user/owner whom says the model in question is stupid, lazy, dumb, idiotic, a jerk, crazy and anything else they may come up with. The user/owner can also deny saying anything of the sort. It is the user/owners byguidelines set forth as in the charter.

DEAN

CHIPS, MODULES, AND SENSORS
Some if not all chips, modules and/or circuits
listed in the order they are used sometimes.

LIAR—Limited Interactive Alertness Retardation
EGO—Electronic Genetic Organ
EAT—Emotional And Timely
ETC—Emotional Trauma Chip
ATTITUDE—Automatic Threat Transducing
Independent Timed Universal Delayed Emitter
DIMWIT—Delayed Integrated Module With
Instant Termination
DICK—Digital Interactive Circuit Kicker
GAS—General Alert System
CARE—Compatibility And Resource Engine
TIRED—Tranquilized Individual Response
Emergency Diagnostic

SPECIAL NOTE: If by the time you have
reached this mark, you should be totally crazy,
terminally insane or possibly even have a better
insight into how unstable models are. By
successfully reading this manual you now know
what it is like to be in the mind of a man. A man

created for one purpose. Work, Pay Bills and become enslaved by the user/owner.

GLOSSARY
(WARNING)
It is up to the reader on what these terms may
mean if they have any meaning

GODthority--The one you pray to.
Transducing--Reduces the alertness level.
Psychoanalyctical--Just a term for this book.
Shotline--What you hear in the bar.
Byguidelines--Something made up.
Acquirization--When you acquire the license for.

THE REAL MEANING OF MEN

As you may have guessed, there really is no true meaning to what men do or can do or even want to do. They are complicated and cannot be evaluated in any other way than to actually interact and see if the model of choice is adaptable to your desires/neeeds. We don't mean a lot of the things we say as you must also understand when we say something you the female usually takes it the wrong way, any way. We have to apologize, as men are difficult and sometimes not all there.

A man's feelings usually tend to get pushed aside, as they can see something bigger and better somewhere in the future. Most times when they get involved with someone, they are true to them, but not all men are created equal. If they were you wouldn't have a choice. Choices are what make us all different than each other.

It is hard to predict what any man at any given time will do. They all react differently and they all had different teachers in life. Even if they had all the same things and looked the same way, they would still be different. Men tend to be shy or straightforward and sometimes they beat around the bush. They are as complicated as they make themselves, and when you add any element, they change.

Sometimes, the changes are good and sometimes they aren't. It all depends on each person individually. There is no true way to evaluate any one person using any method and expect to get certain results. It is impossible to tell whether one model is different than any other. Motors and mechanical things, they can be evaluated because they actually do, do the same function with no errors except breakage and bad things going wrong.

There will be times when you think you know what a man is like. You are in denial. No one, not even the man himself can tell you much about any other man they know. A few details, but that is the way men retain their information. Differently than each other and any other human. The more they know the more complicated they become.

No man has any more of an idea of what they are thinking. Sometimes and rather often the mouth engages long before the brain. In these instances don't take what man says as a given. They may mean something totally different than what you think. Men often don't think before they speak. It is just a flaw in the design of men.

Men are much more than most give them credit for. When a man falls in love he will devote as much time to the one he loves. He often will make sacrifices that change him. When a counterpart decides they want someone different than what they have, they try changing the model. There can be adverse reactions and effects that most would rather not deal with.

These experiences are what makes a man what he is. Most, if not some change how they grew up. Some and most, if not all are swayed into a set of beliefs that may not be right. Each model has to decide which way they are going to allow their minds and decisions to be swayed.

Men are and always will be unpredictable, unreliable, unclear and/or uncontrollable. Their actions may not be sane and in some cases may even become unstable or even erratic. No one test can decipher what a man really is. Men also treat most problems whether they are mechanical and/or emotional as if it were fixable.

Men often can fix what the problem(s) may be. Men just need to know where they stand in order to be a better person for all around. There are some, if quite a few exceptions to some and/or all the rules. These are the most cunning, sly models you will find. They are devious and possibly dangerous. Most if not some of them do have mental issues long before they interacted with anyone else.

There is limited insight that any book or professional can give about the real meaning of what and who a man is. The variations for each individual man vary, as each experience is different. It is similar to a roller coaster that changes every time you ride it. The next ride will be different but it may also be scarier or not quite so scary.

Some of the men you encounter in your journey, are not quite what you expect. There are some out there that have no good intentions but because of one or two, everyone seems to think that all men are like that. Not true. As is found in most things done, just because one or two are bad doesn't make the whole basket bad.

It could be the upbringing. It could be the way we were taught to interpret things by influence. It could be the way life treated us and some of the models took it to heart. Some just took it. And some just couldn't deal with it because they were limited in their thinking ability. Each man interprets things differently, as do women, (please see Manual 2 Women for further insight into this phenomenon).

Some men have strange thoughts and yes it seems funny in the mind, but if you say it, it will definitely sound stupid. And in most cases when it is blurted out, the man telling the story will laugh but no one else will. User/owners who encounter this may not like what they hear and may even inadvertently call said model names because it sounds stupid.

Men are not like anything else you may encounter. They have different emotional values than most. Some are complicated only in the fact they have no basic common sense. Some may be smart but as stupid as a box of rocks when it comes to something so simple.

Man is as difficult to figure out as anything as complicated as manly emotions and/or the lack thereof. Some if any model may not be evaluated properly and any of their actions could possibly be misconstrued or mistaken for something other than the intended results.

For many years, many people have tried to figure why a man thinks the way he does. It is irrational and irresponsible at most times. When a man thinks he doesn't know at most all times what he is thinking or why he has thought what he has thought.

No one person can say with any clarity or truth what makes a man tick besides love, lust, toys, fun, domination, pervertedness, strangeness or just anything that may activate the wrong side effects. Man is as complicated as any machine with 12 million parts and counting.

Some men have a lot of stamina and willpower and these men tend to be in the construction field. Occasionally you will find one in the office. Some have strong mental processes. These tend to find themselves at home with executive jobs. They tend to have more idiosyncratic behavior.

Some men make lots of money while others starve to death. Some men are born rich and others earn it. Some are born poor and make themselves a life worth living. Some have crazy tendencies and may exhibit odd and unusual behavior.

As men go through their lives, they encounter many problems and obstacles. When they reach these things, reactions and actions tend to differ. Not many make the same decision and none make the exact same choices. As each decision and reaction to any problem minor or major can and will result in man making a different choice for himself.

As he makes these choices they drastically change and alter his current life. His mood may change. His demeanor may alter and go berserk at times. His mentality may also be altered as the choices they make alter the life they live.

DEAN

I have found through living life as a man, that we are all different and no two can be evaluated by any certain criteria. Life in its entirety may be hazardous and dangerous to any other human or animal that may inadvertently interact with any model of today or yesterday. Men will not be figured out because of the complexities involved. If it were that easy, men wouldn't be men anymore.

Most men feel they want to be with someone, but when that someone doesn't appreciate what they have, then men are no longer worthwhile to be interacted with. Most men may feel a degree of hope, faith, love and trust for any female model with whom they interact with.

As crazy as men can be at times, it is the women who bring it out and release the nasty man who was hiding inside the shell. Some men are very adamant about wanting to give a woman the benefit of the doubt and to be trusting to those women. As is in all and most all cases, woman in general cannot appreciate nor do what is right by man.

Man cannot be evaluated or diagnosed by any single person or being. They become protective of their own life and when they feel threatened the one who threatens them is responsible for the actions they have caused by doing what they do. Men are difficult but that is only to be expected.

A man has problems from the time they can talk and walk. After that it just gets more complicated and much more difficult to understand the way they think and the actions they provide. Some and most all actions are negotiable when it comes to love and the matter of love. Man was not built to withstand multiple interactions with other humans except as noted above and/or below.

Men are created with certain predilections for life. Once the woman has altered their way of thinking and living the man is and always will be very difficult to deal with and be around. Women unknowingly think that just because a man is with them, then they must change them to what they want.

What is essentially good for a woman is definitely not good for a man. Men differ in structure as well as lifestyles and women tend to change that. Once the change has begun the man must either hope for the best or give in to the woman.

Woman change and want the man to change with her but unerringly the man may suffer and the woman may hinder his life. By thinking a man is exactly like a woman, the man will suffer for it and then the consequences are the responsibility of the woman who changed him. No man can be altered in the way of woman. When he is, anything can and always will happen.

Men tend to hold themselves to a higher standard than women do. Women think they can control the man, but it is difficult and once changed cannot be undone. The man, when he experiences certain things cannot unchange what they learned. There are varying degrees from normal to totally and absolutely bonkers. They begin life normal and the interactions they encounter may drive them bonkers.

When women encounter men and interact with them, why can they not leave the man alone and allow him to become himself instead of changing who they are? Because a woman does not want to change her life without changing his life in the process.

All models have an invariably different sensor input and output interface. Not all the models you encounter may have any and/or all sensory inputs. The sensory inputs are different and may require additional treatment when in doubt.

Please consult General Ovulational Dynamix or GOD for more information regarding this office.

ADDITIONAL EXCLUSIONS AND/OR LIMITATIONS

Due to unforeseen risks, no part of this manual may be read in its entirety unless otherwise noted in any section or sub-section of any book published since before time or long after. No part of this manual may be printed in part or in whole. This manual is copyrighted and falls under the anti-piracy laws that may apply where you live. Some laws do not apply when applied correctly. If you feel you have read this manual in error, please report to your nearest service center for assistance.

This manual in no way implies that there actually is a service center anywhere. Men are not for sale and may only be purchased from an authorized bar representative. Some bars are not legal and you therefore may have inadvertently purchased a defective model. No model may be held for ransom or reason under any circumstances. If you feel you have reached your man in error please call our 24-hour shotline. By 24 hour we mean 24 hours in a day for GOD. We may not be open when you need us most. We were open at the beginning of time for the first 24 hours and haven't been since.

Limitations for certain models may be purchased separately at your nearest bookstore or yard sale, possibly. There is a limited time in which any user/owner may contact a service center for a full refund. During this time there is a 45-year waiting list for quality interaction purposes. In this case you must wait 45 years until you are allowed a refund. If anything major happens in this time there is no refund available and you may be responsible for anything that goes wrong until such time as is required by the warranty.

Any and all limitations and/or exclusions may not be transferred to any party without prior disclosure of the limitations and/or exclusions. When transferring ownership to another user/owner only the most active user/owner may qualify for assistance. If, however, the model was traded and/or given away as a gift then no warranty may be implied. Some and most all models have been given a once over before they were created and quality control may be responsible for any and all limitations and/or exclusions.

In any of these cases you must report to the quality control office located in a suburb off another drive in another part of the galaxy. Some offices may be closed due to unforeseen downsizing purposes. During the interaction period there will be no warranties as implied in any form or in any part of this manual.

The only model covered by this manual and with no limitations and/or exclusions and with full lifetime warranty was discontinued during the beginning when it was exclusive to society. To find out if your model is the one that is covered, please consult a professional near you who may know if your model is covered.

When possible, the limitations and/or exclusions may not be limited or excluded. When the limitations on any model is given, it will be labeled accordingly. Some exclusions may not be exclusive to your model. When models are excluded from the limitations listed herein it is up to the user/owner to be certain the model in question is excluded from the limitations.

When any model is excluded from any activity it requires to interact with others, the user/owner can be found negligent on any part of the listed offenses located in Manual 3 Everything In Between. No user/owner may exclude any model from the limitations or exclusions listed herein and therefore may be responsible and held accountable for these crimes against man.

No user/owner may exclude any model from any activity that the user/owner sees fit to exclude them from. The user/owner cannot limit the model(s) for any reason other than trading purposes. When excluding any model from any activity or requirement as listed, the user/owner is responsible for the actions caused by these exclusions and/or limitations.

MISCELLANEOUS THOUGHTS

Understanding a man can be as difficult as learning to fly a super jet and playing a game of chess and texting to a friend all while sleeping. If you can do this, you can understand a man. For all others who read this manual, you might be pleasantly surprised. Some of the stuff in this manual is pretty good basic information. Some of it is made up.

But that is also what a man really is. Difficult at times. Hard to understand. Not too clearly defined. They know what to say, well at least a lot of them do, but they have the capability to confuse a partner so much as to get them to date him. Men are just horndogs at most all times.

The few who are not quite all there are an exception and you should not label all men in any one category. They differ on all aspects as snowflakes do. No 2 are alike and no 2 can ever be the same. Except in cases where scientists have decided they can clone anything.

Men try figuring things out and how they work and what it takes to fix it. If men can fix the problem, then what is the problem? You should not take lightly what you say to a man and do not misinterpret what he means when he says what he says.

Some would call them crazy or just strange. But most times when someone hears something, then his partner can take it in a totally different way in which it was said, could be a misrepresentation on the part of the one misunderstanding. If you aren't sure what the man means when he says something, just ask. We aren't terrible people. We can be compassionate and romantic yet firm and someone to lean on.

Men can be as difficult and extremely misunderstood but not as much as a woman could be. For more information on this please get Manual 2 Woman. Men sometimes do... Well actually quite often, think with the wrong part of the body. But some would say this is the way to a man's heart.

Men can be very complicated and when placed with a partner, he may be uncontrollable. But, they can be tamed. All it takes is the right partner to interact with them and if they hit it off and are compatible, then maybe they should pursue relations. Just remember there will be fights big and small. When in doubt remember why you fell in love with the man. As long as you remember this, you will stay in love.

Try not to change the man too much. They can and will be rebellious if changed too much. Men can change but they prefer a more uncomplicated life. Men try to be relaxed at most times but stress can become inherent if they let it. Once a man starts stressing a lot, changing them can be disturbing to say the least. They do like routines but can be spontaneous if they know whether the partner they are with lets them know what they like and dislike.

Men are and always will be into excitement and adventure. New things that intrigue them and this is up to the partner of the man to determine what he may like and/or dislike. All men are different and they deserve a second chance, as do their partners. We all make mistakes and yes, men hate admitting a mistake, but will. They swallow their pride and confess to the errors of their ways. But if they feel threatened by revealing this, they may try to keep it quiet. If found out, yes they will admit to it then.

A man does need someone they can hang out with at times. Someone they can talk to and possibly get a little advice from. That is why men go fishing, to the bar, 4X4ing, dart leagues, bowling leagues, boating and just being with someone they can trust. When a man trusts someone, they expect anything that's said to be kept private and confidential.

A man does like to be backed up by their partner, as he will do for them. If a man feels their partner doesn't back them up or stand behind them, then a problem may and possibly will occur. A man can be hazardous at times, but most will not do anything they feel is dangerous. Most often a man may look like he is doing something dangerous but it is only as dangerous as the man doing it.

Man tends to be observant and well intentioned when interacting becomes a problem for the user/owner. If this is the case with your model, you may want to return it to the place of purchase for future endeavors, only it can determine by the interactions it so chooses.

Man should keep his mouth shut, as anything they say can and will be used totally against them from the moment they make the errant words. Man does become accustomed to a partner controlling them, provided the partner has no ill begotten intentions.

Any partner who points out any toy a man may desire, is required to offer said toy to man and not be teased with the ill intentioned mentioning of said toy. Man will always be a difficult but easy to understand individual if partner has the knowledge and the intelligence to completely understand them.

Man can and always could possibly be aggressive when placed in any situation they feel threatened by. In work mode, a man will and could possibly be wanting something better but may not require it, unless challenged by any model that has been released.

Man in a partnership mode may not speak as much in the future of the relationship(s) it so chooses to pursue and this could accidentally trigger an unwanted reaction from any and/or all partners. Partners vary by size, shape and model and may not be predetermined by anyone so willing to try and understand what a man really is and could be.

No one man can be labeled or stereotyped no matter what path the man may so choose. Choosing different paths and futures is what makes the man a formidable ally or enemy. If any interaction causes any path to be taken that was not intended, then any and/or all models may be at the mercy of any partner they are currently involved with.

Each model acts independently from all other models available. When a man can be predicted, the model in question may change or alter its programming at any time without any notice or advance warning. If and when this may actually happen, be patient and do not stand in their way. As the new programming takes effect the user and/or owner should make mental notes of all the changes they have witnessed and return the report to any and all service centers.

During any interaction with any human, any model may exhibit different attitudes and ever changing dilemmas. These may not be trusted except as specified in any charter currently available.

A man may or may not like anyone he may encounter. A man can learn to live around people they really don't like, as most are equipped with certain core values and emotions. Other men just seem to be lacking something or maybe they have a different set of core values entirely.

The emotions a man may display, may or may not be as accurate as the look on his face. Men do tend to most often and sometimes always display the facial results but not in the way they were intended to be displayed. You must forgive us for this. We did not ask for it but we got stuck with it. Whatever it may possibly maybe be.

A man can be manipulated but not totally against his will, except in certain cases. Man tends to like to be someone of value to someone somewhere. Sometimes a man may decide a sport is his mate and he spends all his time and money on the sport collecting memorabilia and such. Some find someone to latch onto and this is not a bad thing.

To evaluate or even try to evaluate a man could possibly violate one or more laws somewhere. Men can cope without a partner, but most all, if not some do like the companionship of someone they can integrate with. There can be no set examples or any type of guideline for any man who is ever born or ever will be born, except as noted in the cloned models guide.

MISCELLANEOUS

Man can seem like a predictable human but in most all cases, man is tougher to break than diamonds. Unfortunately, by the time most figure this out, they are too old to care. No 2 men can be given the exact same test, as the results will differ as men will as well. Man has a good side and a bad side and some have an evil side.

The most common mistake most others make, is thinking they know what a man is thinking. But the foolery begins as soon as the boy learns to learn and decide for himself. Once the boy has reached adulthood, he has learned many things and can be totally unaware at times of his actions.

A man's behavior changes always and whenever he can, to suit his needs. His needs have always been a forefront memory and when the man can change for himself he does. Unfortunately at times, the man is incapable of even the most simplest of answers. A man can become confused if given too many orders/demands/askances at one time or in any order.

www.ingramcontent.com/pod-product-compliance
Lightning Source LLC
Chambersburg PA
CBHW070548030426
42337CB00016B/2408